CONTENTS

ABOUT THE ONLINE AUDIO

On the title page of this book you will find a code that allows you to access the online audio tracks. You can listen to these online or download them to your computer and/or mobile device. To hear a given etude, refer to its number; the online audio track is named accordingly (e.g., Etude 21 = Track 21).

The tracks for "Night Rider" and five additional play-along tracks are given below.

PLAY-ALONG TRACKS

TRACK 176 • **Night Rider** (demo)

TRACK 177 • **Night Rider** (play-along)

TRACK 178 • **Flying in D**

TRACK 179 • **Flying in G**

TRACK 180 • **Flying in C**

TRACK 181 • **Flying in A**

TRACK 182 • **Learning to Fly in D**

FOREWORD

Welcome to *Rockin' Strings*! Here is the chance to enter the new world of playing today's music while learning to express your own music through improvisation. Don't be afraid! *Rockin' Strings* is going to lead you step-by-step. We begin at home with the D major scale and then teach you how to create your own melodies and tunes one step at a time. Play along with the accompanying audio tracks. They will make you sound like a star as you begin to progress through the book, exploring additional keys and rhythms while improvising – all in the style of popular music. Play by yourself, with your teacher, your friends, and your school orchestra.

Teachers, jump in. Even though you may not improvise regularly, *Rockin' Strings* will lead you right along with the students. Be brave! Trust us. You will be safe using *Rockin' Strings* in your string classes and studios. Easy to understand and designed for success, you and your students will now have a way to complement our great classical solo and school orchestra repertoire. *Rockin' Strings* will introduce your students to a new genre of music and creativity, using their string instruments to reinforce the great playing foundation you are giving them. Plus, bringing today's music into your studio or classroom may attract even more attention to strings in your schools and community.

During the last few years we have pilot tested *Rockin' Strings* with over 250 teachers and over 500 intermediate string students. The pedagogy is streamlined, sequential, with unison melodies, duets, and arrangements, all incorporating a carefully structured sequence for learning how to improvise successfully for both you and your students. This gives students the opportunity to create their own music through improvisation, transfer their playing skills from classical to improvising and back again, develop independent musicianship, and have some fun – while getting even more excited about playing a string instrument.

Teachers of all different backgrounds have found success with *Rockin' Strings.* I am confident that you will, too. I strongly support the work of Mark Wood and *Rockin' Strings.* Mark has introduced me to the world of improvising with rock 'n' roll music, and I have had the pleasure of bringing string pedagogy for students to Mark. As a music educator, I was happy to contribute some musical advice to this publication.

Are you ready for new musical experiences? Grab your instrument. Turn on the audio tracks and get started. The world of today's music, along with making your own, is waiting for you. *Rockin' Strings* is the door. Open it and get flying!

Dr. Robert Gillespie, violinist

Professor of Music, Ohio State University
Co-author, *Essential Elements for Strings*
publ. Hal Leonard Corporation

ROCKIN' STRINGS

IMPROV LESSONS & TIPS FOR THE CONTEMPORARY PLAYER

BY MARK WOOD

FOREWORD BY DR. ROBERT GILLESPIE

To access audio online, visit:
www.halleonard.com/mylibrary

Enter Code
7712-9053-8449-9651

PLAYBACK+
Speed • Pitch • Balance • Loop

Cover art by Albert Oh

All music composed and performed by Mark Wood.

Mark Wood – 7-string Viper violin
Elijah Wood – drums
Rob Bambach – guitar
Paul Ranieri – bass

ISBN 978-1-4950-9373-9

7777 W. BLUEMOUND RD. P.O. BOX 13819 MILWAUKEE, WI 53213

In Australia Contact:
Hal Leonard Australia Pty. Ltd.
4 Lentara Court
Cheltenham, Victoria, 3192 Australia
Email: ausadmin@halleonard.com.au

Visit Hal Leonard Online at
www.halleonard.com

INTRODUCTION

How to Use This Book

This method introduces a set of improvisational adventures designed to explore the wondrous world of your students' imagination and their interaction with music making. Each stage in the book builds on the progression of the learning curve, from easy to more challenging.

It is important that we teach improvising. Not only is it required in the National Standards of Music Teaching, but it also empowers the student to "find" themselves in their chosen instrument, enabling the formation of a lifelong bond to the joy of music. If you, the teacher, are new to improvising, we encourage you to participate alongside the students. The call-and-response part of the book is important for additional ear training and for freedom of instantaneous expression. Invent your own melodies to pass back and forth from teacher to student. Since music is a language skill, have a spontaneous musical conversation every day!

Clear intonation and rhythmic accuracy are the two biggest challenges for string players. Recognizing this, the play-along tracks were set up as an ear-empowering exercise. Each track was composed to the highest standards of music production, by adding great live musicians and by a strong commitment to melody. As you approach each etude, always use the play-along tracks, so the students can anchor onto the drone to reinforce intonation and anchor to the loops for rhythmic acuity. It would be a good idea to place all the audio tracks onto an iPad or computer to loop and control each example. Additionally, Hal Leonard's *PLAYBACK+* is a multifunctional audio player that allows you to slow down audio without changing pitch, set loop points, change keys, and pan left or right.

The basic major, minor, pentatonic, and modal scales are covered in this book. As you deem appropriate, share with your students any additional scale information, showing them how to apply the scales to improvisation.

Finally, the last song, "Night Rider," is a performance piece that can be played at any event, showcasing the depth of your students' expression and their commitment to owning the music for themselves. Their voice matters!

I would like to thank Dr. Robert Gillespie for partnering with me on this wonderful project of bringing strings into the 21st century. He is a great musician and truly is the Yoda of string pedagogy. Likewise, I owe a debt of gratitude to Elizabeth Petersen for the cello pedagogy, to Aaron Yackley for the double bass pedagogy, and to everyone at Ohio State University for their support of future string teachers.

–Mark Wood

STAGE 1
The Building Blocks of Improvisation
D Major

BUILDING BLOCKS
1. D Major Scale

2. D Major Arpeggio

3. D Major

4. FOLLOW THE LEADER

Improvisation
Use the rhythm indicated. Choose any notes in the first two measures to play.

5. UNDERCOVER

Improvisation
Use the rhythm indicated. Choose any notes in the first two measures to play.

6. MOVING ON

Improvisation
Use the rhythm indicated. Choose any notes in the first two measures to play.

7. RUN JUMP

Improvisation
Use the rhythm indicated. Choose any notes in the first two measures to play.

8. FEEL THE TWO

Improvisation
Use the rhythm indicated. Choose any notes in the first two measures to play.

9. TWO FOR TWO

Improvisation
Use the rhythm indicated. Choose any notes in the first two measures to play.

Emphasizing beats 2 and 4
Body movement: Rock back and forth with the beat while playing.

10. TWO PLUS FOUR

11. FOUR WITH TWO

12A. TWICE AS FUN (Duet A)

Be careful of these rests.

Be careful of these rests.

12B. TWICE AS FUN (Duet B)

3

D Major and B Minor

BUILDING BLOCKS
B Minor Scale

13. STREETS OF NYC
B minor

Improvisation
Use the rhythm indicated. Choose any notes in the first two measures to play.

14. HOME BASE
B minor

Improvisation

15. ONE WHEEL
B minor

Improvisation

16. FAR AND WIDE
B minor

Improvisation

17. CLIMB
D major

Improvisation

18. TALK THE TALK
D major

Improvisation

19. ANSWER
D major

Improvisation

20. VIOLETS ARE BLUE
D major

Improvisation (2 bars)

D Major

G Major

G Major and E Minor

BUILDING BLOCKS
E Minor Scale

39. STREETS OF NYC
E minor

(Use any rhythm.)
Improvisation

40. NIGHT SKY
E minor

Improvisation

41. ONE WHEEL
E minor

Improvisation

42. FAR AND WIDE
E minor

Improvisation

43. GOING HOME
G major

Improvisation

44. TALK THE TALK
G major

Improvisation

45. ANSWER
G major

Improvisation

46. STRUT
G major

Improvisation (2 bars)

47. WALK THAT WAY
G major

Improvisation

5

Improvisation

C Major

C Major and A Minor

BUILDING BLOCKS
A Minor Scale

57. EYES ARE DEEP
A minor

(Use any rhythm.)
Improvisation

58. RAIN
A minor

Improvisation

59. GLIMMER
A minor

Improvisation

60. FAR AND WIDE
A minor

Improvisation

61. SUNRISE
C major

Improvisation

62. TALK THE TALK
C major

Improvisation

63. ANSWER
C major

Improvisation

64. VIOLETS ARE BLUE
C major

Improvisation (2 bars)

A Major

A Major and F♯ Minor

BUILDING BLOCKS
F♯ Minor Scale

74. SNOW FOX
F♯ minor

Improvisation

75. OIL AND WATER
F♯ minor

Improvisation

76. FAR AND WIDE
F♯ minor

Improvisation

77. DARK TO LIGHT
F♯ minor

Improvisation

78. ONE WHEEL
A major

Improvisation

79. ANSWER
A major

Improvisation

80. KICK START
A major

Improvisation

81. VIOLETS ARE BLUE
A major

Improvisation (2 bars)

STAGE 2
Intervals

OCTAVES
82. ON ALL STRINGS

83. OCTAVES WITH 8th NOTES

84. SKIP JUMP

85. INTERVALS

86. G MAJOR SCALE IN THIRDS

87. G MAJOR SCALE IN FOURTHS

88. G MAJOR SCALE IN FIFTHS

STAGE 3
Major Pentatonic Scales with Improvisation

D Major Pentatonic

14

95. CALL/RESPONSE

suggested: 4   2 4 - 4

II   I
A string

G Major Pentatonic

96. G Major Pentatonic Scale

97. G Major Pentatonic Scale (lowest note to highest note in 1st position)

98. JUMP UP

Improvisation

99. SMILE

Improvisation

100. COUNTRY FEEL

Improvisation (2 bars)

101. STRAW HAT

Improvisation (2 bars)

C Major Pentatonic

102. C Major Pentatonic Scale

103. C Major Pentatonic Scale (lowest note to highest note in 1st position)

104. JUMP

105. SMILE

106. COUNTRY FEEL

107. STRAW HAT

A Major Pentatonic

108. A Major Pentatonic Scale

109. A Major Pentatonic Scale (lowest note to highest note in 1st position)

110. JUMP

Improvisation

111. SMILE

Improvisation

112. COUNTRY FEEL

Improvisation (2 bars)

113. STRAW HAT

Improvisation (2 bars)

Syncopation

114. CALL AND RESPONSE

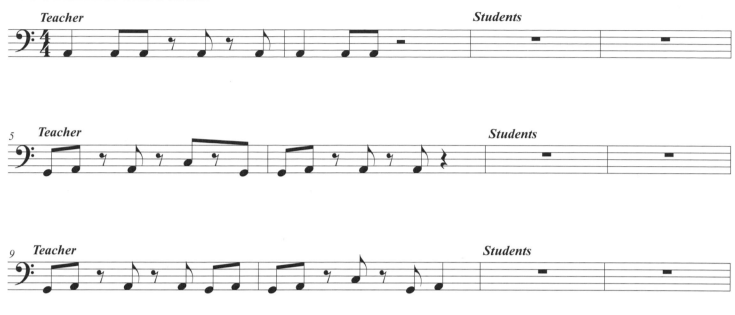

STAGE 4
Learning to Fly in D Major

MUSICAL TOOL KIT TO CREATE YOUR OWN MUSIC
D Major Pentatonic Scale

Rhythmic Ideas

115. LEARNING TO FLY (2-bar solo)

Improvisation (2 bars)
*(Choose any notes and rhythms from
the first two lines at the top of the page.)*

116. LEARNING TO FLY (4-bar solo)

Improvisation (4 bars)
(Choose any notes and rhythms from the first two lines at the top of the page.)

Learning to Fly in G Major

MUSICAL TOOL KIT TO CREATE YOUR OWN MUSIC
G Major Pentatonic Scale

Rhythmic Ideas

117. LEARNING TO FLY (2-bar solo)

Improvisation (2 bars)
(Choose any notes and rhythms from the first two lines at the top of the page.)

118. LEARNING TO FLY (4-bar solo)

Improvisation (4 bars)
(Choose any notes and rhythms from the first two lines at the top of the page.)

Learning to Fly in C Major

MUSICAL TOOL KIT TO CREATE YOUR OWN MUSIC
C Major Pentatonic Scale

Rhythmic Ideas

119. LEARNING TO FLY (2-bar solo)

Improvisation (2 bars)
(Choose any notes and rhythms from
the first two lines at the top of the page.)

120. LEARNING TO FLY (4-bar solo)

Improvisation (4 bars)
(Choose any notes and rhythms from the first two lines at the top of the page.)

Learning to Fly in A Major

MUSICAL TOOL KIT TO CREATE YOUR OWN MUSIC
A Major Pentatonic Scale

Rhythmic Ideas

121. LEARNING TO FLY (2-bar solo)

Improvisation (2 bars)
(Choose any notes and rhythms from
the first two lines at the top of the page.)

122. LEARNING TO FLY (4-bar solo)

Improvisation (4 bars)
(Choose any notes and rhythms from
the first two lines at the top of the page.)

STAGE 5
Flying in D Major

D Major Pentatonic Scale

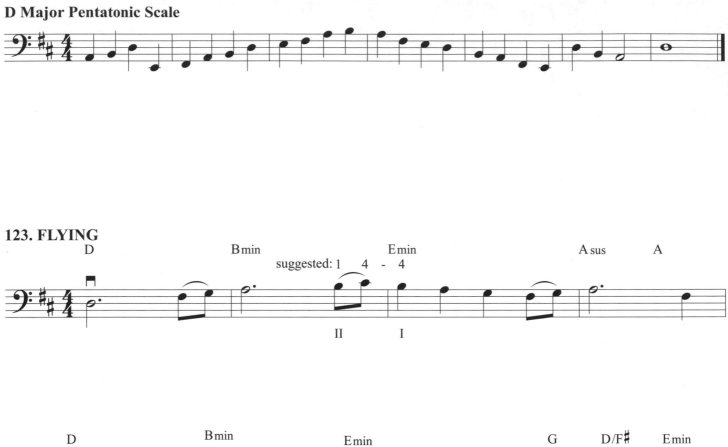

123. FLYING

Improv with the D major pentatonic scale.
Choose your notes from the scale at the top of page 24.
Use any rhythms you want when you improv.

Improv with the D major pentatonic scale.
Choose your notes from the scale at the top of page 24.
Use any rhythms you want when you improv.

Flying in G Major

G Major Pentatonic Scale

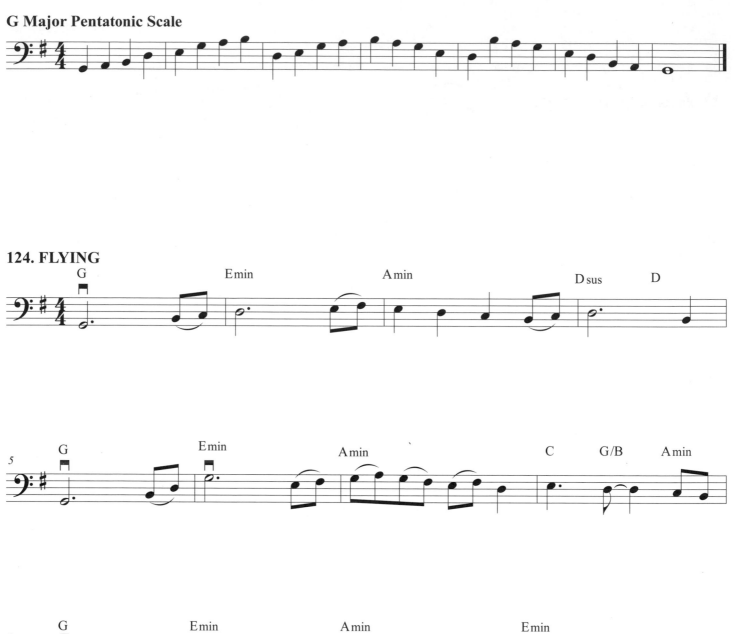

124. FLYING

Flying in C Major

Improv with the C major pentatonic scale.
Choose your notes from the scale at the top of page 28.
Use any rhythms you want when you improv.

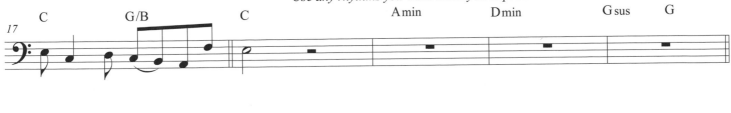

Improv with the C major pentatonic scale.
Choose your notes from the scale at the top of page 28.
Use any rhythms you want when you improv.

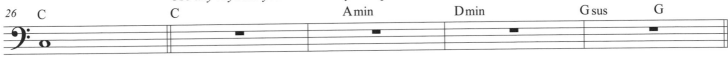

Flying in A Major

STAGE 6
Pentatonic Scales & Blues Scales

B Minor Pentatonic/Blues Scales

127. B Minor Pentatonic Scale

128. B Minor Pentatonic Scale (lowest note to highest note in 1st position)

129. DEEP THOUGHT

Improvisation

130. STEP BY STEP

Improvisation

131. DOWN AND UP

Improvisation

132. REACH THE TOP

Improvisation

133. B Minor Blues Scale

134. B Minor Blues Scale (2 octaves)

135. IN SIGHT   *Improvisation*

136. CRY OUT   *Improvisation*

137. NIGHT LIGHTS   *Improvisation*

138. GLOW   *Improvisation*

E Minor Pentatonic/Blues Scales

139. E Minor Pentatonic Scale

140. E Minor Pentatonic Scale (lowest note to highest note in 1st position)

141. DEEP THOUGHT

Improvisation

142. STEP BY STEP

Improvisation

143. DOWN AND UP

Improvisation

144. REACH THE TOP

Improvisation

A Minor Pentatonic/Blues Scales

151. A Minor Pentatonic Scale

152. A Minor Pentatonic Scale (lowest note to highest note in 1st position)

153. DEEP THOUGHT   *Improvisation*

154. STEP BY STEP   *Improvisation*

155. DOWN AND UP   *Improvisation*

156. REACH THE TOP   *Improvisation*

157. A Minor Blues Scale

158. A Minor Blues Scale (2 octaves)

159. IN SIGHT   *Improvisation*

160. CRY OUT   *Improvisation*

161. NIGHT LIGHTS   *Improvisation*

162. GLOW   *Improvisation*

F♯ Minor Pentatonic/Blues Scales

163. F♯ Minor Pentatonic Scale

164. F♯ Minor Pentatonic Scale (lowest note to highest note in 1st position)

165. DEEP THOUGHT

Improvisation

166. STEP BY STEP

Improvisation

167. DOWN AND UP

Improvisation

168. REACH THE TOP

Improvisation

169. F♯ Minor Blues Scale

170. F♯ Minor Blues Scale (2 octaves)

171. IN SIGHT

Improvisation

172. CRY OUT

Improvisation

173. NIGHT LIGHTS

Improvisation

174. GLOW

Improvisation

STAGE 7
Blues Shuffle in A Minor

A Minor Blues Scale

(pizz. optional)

175. Blues Shuffle with Triplets

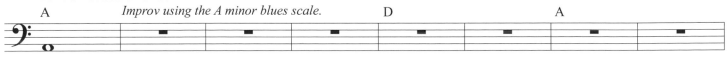

12-bar blues chords

STAGE 8
Night Rider

By Mark Wood

Night Rider

By Mark Wood

Improv using the A min pentatonic scale

ABOUT THE AUTHOR

Photo by Maryanne Bilham

Recording artist, performer, producer, inventor, Emmy-winning composer and music education advocate Mark Wood has spent the past four decades electrifying the orchestra industry – literally.

Dubbed "The Les Paul of the Violin World" by PBS, the Juilliard-trained violinist first turned the string establishment on its head in the early 1970s with his invention of the first solid-body electric violin. His company, Wood Violins, is the premier manufacturer of electric violins, violas, and cellos worldwide. Mark holds the patent for the first-ever self-supporting violin.

Wood is a world-renowned performer who rose to fame as string master and founding member of the internationally acclaimed Trans-Siberian Orchestra. A successful solo artist in his own right, Wood writes and records original music for film and television, has released six solo albums, and tours with his band The Mark Wood Experience (MWE), which features his wife, vocalist Laura Kaye, and their drummer son Elijah. His commission credits include The Juilliard School and extensive TV broadcast music including The Winter Olympics and The Tour de France (for which he won an Emmy).

In addition to his continued solo and commission work, Wood has collaborated with and appeared alongside some of the biggest names in music, such as Lenny Kravitz, Celine Dion, and Kanye West. As a member of his touring band, Wood had the honor of performing with the legendary Billy Joel for both historic final concerts at Shea stadium, sharing the stage with Paul McCartney, Steven Tyler, and Roger Daltry. He also starred in a Kanye West-produced national Pepsi TV commercial and has appeared on the world's most venerable stages, including Carnegie Hall, Lincoln Center, and Madison Square Garden.

But his true passion is music education. His program Electrify Your Strings (EYS) – now in its 15th year – is an intensive rock-and-roll workshop for school music education departments that boosts student self-esteem and motivation and helps raise money for music education. Today EYS visits upward of 60 schools per year. The organization has been featured on *The Today Show* and *CBS Evening News* and in countless local media outlets.

But for Wood, it's all about the kids. He's dedicated to providing educators with the opportunity to ignite their students' passions and to inspiring students to open their minds and unlock their potential. His book *Electrify Your Strings: The Mark Wood Improvisational Violin Method* is regarded as the definitive electric violin method book. The first in a series of forthcoming educational books, Wood is passionate about providing educators and students with the tools they need to succeed in the classroom and beyond.

HAL•LEONARD INSTRUMENTAL PLAY-ALONG

Your favorite songs are arranged just for solo instrumentalists with this outstanding series. Each book includes a great full-accompaniment play-along audio so you can sound just like a pro! Check out **www.halleonard.com** to see all the titles available.

The Beatles

All You Need Is Love • Blackbird • Day Tripper • Eleanor Rigby • Get Back • Here, There and Everywhere • Hey Jude • I Will • Let It Be • Lucy in the Sky with Diamonds • Ob-La-Di, Ob-La-Da • Penny Lane • Something • Ticket to Ride • Yesterday.

_____00225330	Flute	$14.99
_____00225331	Clarinet	$14.99
_____00225332	Alto Sax	$14.99
_____00225333	Tenor Sax	$14.99
_____00225334	Trumpet	$14.99
_____00225335	Horn	$14.99
_____00225336	Trombone	$14.99
_____00225337	Violin	$14.99
_____00225338	Viola	$14.99
_____00225339	Cello	$14.99

Chart Hits

All About That Bass • All of Me • Happy • Radioactive • Roar • Say Something • Shake It Off • A Sky Full of Stars • Someone like You • Stay with Me • Thinking Out Loud • Uptown Funk.

_____00146207	Flute	$12.99
_____00146208	Clarinet	$12.99
_____00146209	Alto Sax	$12.99
_____00146210	Tenor Sax	$12.99
_____00146211	Trumpet	$12.99
_____00146212	Horn	$12.99
_____00146213	Trombone	$12.99
_____00146214	Violin	$12.99
_____00146215	Viola	$12.99
_____00146216	Cello	$12.99

Coldplay

Clocks • Every Teardrop Is a Waterfall • Fix You • In My Place • Lost! • Paradise • The Scientist • Speed of Sound • Trouble • Violet Hill • Viva La Vida • Yellow.

_____00103337	Flute	$12.99
_____00103338	Clarinet	$12.99
_____00103339	Alto Sax	$12.99
_____00103340	Tenor Sax	$12.99
_____00103341	Trumpet	$12.99
_____00103342	Horn	$12.99
_____00103343	Trombone	$12.99
_____00103344	Violin	$12.99
_____00103345	Viola	$12.99
_____00103346	Cello	$12.99

Disney Greats

Arabian Nights • Hawaiian Roller Coaster Ride • It's a Small World • Look Through My Eyes • Yo Ho (A Pirate's Life for Me) • and more.

_____00841934	Flute	$12.99
_____00841935	Clarinet	$12.99
_____00841936	Alto Sax	$12.99
_____00841937	Tenor Sax	$12.95
_____00841938	Trumpet	$12.99
_____00841939	Horn	$12.99
_____00841940	Trombone	$12.95
_____00841941	Violin	$12.99
_____00841942	Viola	$12.99
_____00841943	Cello	$12.99
_____00842078	Oboe	$12.99

Great Themes

Bella's Lullaby • Chariots of Fire • Get Smart • Hawaii Five-O Theme • I Love Lucy • The Odd Couple • Spanish Flea • and more.

_____00842468	Flute	$12.99
_____00842469	Clarinet	$12.99
_____00842470	Alto Sax	$12.99
_____00842471	Tenor Sax	$12.99
_____00842472	Trumpet	$12.99
_____00842473	Horn	$12.99
_____00842474	Trombone	$12.99
_____00842475	Violin	$12.99
_____00842476	Viola	$12.99
_____00842477	Cello	$12.99

Popular Hits

Breakeven • Fireflies • Halo • Hey, Soul Sister • I Gotta Feeling • I'm Yours • Need You Now • Poker Face • Viva La Vida • You Belong with Me • and more.

_____00842511	Flute	$12.99
_____00842512	Clarinet	$12.99
_____00842513	Alto Sax	$12.99
_____00842514	Tenor Sax	$12.99
_____00842515	Trumpet	$12.99
_____00842516	Horn	$12.99
_____00842517	Trombone	$12.99
_____00842518	Violin	$12.99
_____00842519	Viola	$12.99
_____00842520	Cello	$12.99

Songs from Frozen, Tangled and Enchanted

Do You Want to Build a Snowman? • For the First Time in Forever • Happy Working Song • I See the Light • In Summer • Let It Go • Mother Knows Best • That's How You Know • True Love's First Kiss • When Will My Life Begin • and more.

_____00126921	Flute	$14.99
_____00126922	Clarinet	$14.99
_____00126923	Alto Sax	$14.99
_____00126924	Tenor Sax	$14.99
_____00126925	Trumpet	$14.99
_____00126926	Horn	$14.99
_____00126927	Trombone	$14.99
_____00126928	Violin	$14.99
_____00126929	Viola	$14.99
_____00126930	Cello	$14.99

Top Hits

Adventure of a Lifetime • Budapest • Die a Happy Man • Ex's & Oh's • Fight Song • Hello • Let It Go • Love Yourself • One Call Away • Pillowtalk • Stitches • Writing's on the Wall.

_____00171073	Flute	$12.99
_____00171074	Clarinet	$12.99
_____00171075	Alto Sax	$12.99
_____00171106	Tenor Sax	$12.99
_____00171107	Trumpet	$12.99
_____00171108	Horn	$12.99
_____00171109	Trombone	$12.99
_____00171110	Violin	$12.99
_____00171111	Viola	$12.99
_____00171112	Cello	$12.99

Wicked

As Long As You're Mine • Dancing Through Life • Defying Gravity • For Good • I'm Not That Girl • Popular • The Wizard and I • and more.

_____00842236	Flute	$12.99
_____00842237	Clarinet	$12.99
_____00842238	Alto Saxophone	$11.95
_____00842239	Tenor Saxophone	$11.95
_____00842240	Trumpet	$11.99
_____00842241	Horn	$11.95
_____00842242	Trombone	$12.99
_____00842243	Violin	$11.99
_____00842244	Viola	$12.99
_____00842245	Cello	$12.99

Prices, contents, and availability subject to change without notice.
Disney characters and artwork © Disney Enterprises, Inc.

HAL•LEONARD®

0617